AROUND THE HOUSE THAT JACK BUILT

AROUND THE HOUSE THAT JACK BUILT

By Roz Abisch/Illustrated by Boche Kaplan

PARENTS' MAGAZINE PRESS/NEW YORK

Text copyright © 1972 by Roz Abisch
Illustrations copyright © 1972 by Boche Kaplan
All rights reserved
Printed in the United States of America
Library of Congress Catalog Card Number: 70-174606
ISBN: Trade 0-8193-0553-7, Library 0-8193-0554-5

Title II, ESEA
PHASE VIII (1972-73)
Project No. 11-73-320

*For Howard R. Abisch
and Max M. Kaplan*

This is the house
that Jack built.

This is the sun
That shines on the house
   that Jack built.

These are the clouds
that cover the sun
That shines on the house
that Jack built.

This is the rain
   that falls from the clouds
That cover the sun
That shines on the house
   that Jack built.

This is the stream
   that starts to flow
After the rain
   so gentle and slow

Falls from the clouds
   that cover the sun
That shines on the house
   that Jack built.

These are the plants
   that freshen the air
With flowers that bloom
   all fragrant and fair
Fed by the stream
   that starts to flow

After the rain
   so gentle and slow
Falls from the clouds
   that cover the sun
That shines on the house
   that Jack built.

These are the bugs
   that pause to feed
From blossom to leaf
   a feast indeed
Eating the plants
   that freshen the air
With flowers that bloom
   all fragrant and fair
Fed by the stream
   that starts to flow
After the rain
   so gentle and slow
Falls from the clouds
   that cover the sun
That shines on the house
   that Jack built.

These are the creatures
   with skill and speed
That hunt the bugs
   that feast and feed
Eating the plants
   that freshen the air
With flowers that bloom
   all fragrant and fair
Fed by the stream
   that starts to flow
After the rain
   so gentle and slow
Falls from the clouds
   that cover the sun
That shines on the house
   that Jack built.

These are the roots
   of the trees so sound
Roots that reach out
   all around
Through the soil
   to hold the ground
Where all the creatures
   with skill and speed
Hunt the bugs
   that feast and feed
Eating the plants
   that freshen the air
With flowers that bloom
   all fragrant and fair
Fed by the stream
   that starts to flow
After the rain
   so gentle and slow
Falls from the clouds
   that cover the sun
That shines on the house
   that Jack built.

These are the leaves
 of red and gold
That flutter down
 to rot and mold
Under the trees
 so tall and sound
With roots that reach out
 all around
Through the soil
 to hold the ground

Where all the creatures
   with skill and speed
Hunt the bugs
   that feast and feed
Eating the plants
   that freshen the air
With flowers that bloom
   all fragrant and fair

Fed by the stream
   that starts to flow
After the rain
   so gentle and slow
Falls from the clouds
   that cover the sun
That shines on the house
   that Jack built.

These are the worms
   that plow and toil
To change the wet leaves
   into soil
After the leaves
   of red and gold
Have fluttered down
   to rot and mold
Under the trees
   so tall and sound
With roots that reach out
   all around
Through the soil
   to hold the ground
Where all the creatures
   with skill and speed
Hunt the bugs
   that feast and feed
Eating the plants
   that freshen the air
With flowers that bloom
   all fragrant and fair
Fed by the stream
   that starts to flow
After the rain
   so gentle and slow
Falls from the clouds
   that cover the sun
That shines on the house
   that Jack built.

These are the birds
   that search the soil
To catch the worms
   that plow and toil

After the leaves
   of red and gold
Have fluttered down
   to rot and mold
Under the trees
   so tall and sound
With roots that reach out
   all around
Through the soil
   to hold the ground
Where all the creatures
   with skill and speed
Hunt the bugs
   that feast and feed
Eating the plants
   that freshen the air
With flowers that bloom
   all fragrant and fair
Fed by the stream
   that starts to flow
After the rain
   so gentle and slow
Falls from the clouds
   that cover the sun
That shines on the house
   that Jack built.

These are the people
 well aware—
People who think
 and really care
About saving the water
 and soil and air
So all living things
 can thrive — everywhere.

These are the people
   well aware
Who know it's important
   to do their share

To protect the birds
   and preserve the soil

In which the earthworms
   plow and toil

After the leaves
   have fluttered down
To rot and mold
   upon the ground

Under the trees
   so tall and sound
With roots that reach out
   all around
Through the soil
   to hold the ground

Where all the creatures
   with skill and speed

Hunt the bugs
   that feast and feed

Eating the plants
   that freshen the air
With flowers that bloom
   all fragrant and fair

Fed by the stream
   that starts to flow
After the rain
   so gentle and slow
Falls from the clouds

   that cover the sun

That shines on the house
   that Jack built.

ROZ ABISCH and BOCHE KAPLAN had wanted to work on a picture book together ever since they were children, and *Open Your Eyes,* published by Parents' Magazine Press in 1964, was the first realization of that wish. They have had well over a dozen books published since then.

A graduate of Brooklyn College, Roz Abisch has been an advertising copywriter as well as a fashion artist and designer. At present, in addition to writing, she works as a substitute teacher in North Merrick, Long Island, where she lives.

Boche Kaplan has lectured at the Solomon R. Guggenheim Foundation, and her etchings and woodcuts have been exhibited at several graphic arts shows at the Brooklyn Museum. She lives in Oceanside, Long Island, where she is a substitute art teacher.

Title II, ESEA
PHASE VIII (1972-73)
Project No. 11-73-320